EXCAVATING THE SKY:

POEMS

EXCAVATING THE SKY:

POEMS

KONSTANTIN KULAKOV

DIALOGUE FOUNDATION BOOKS
SILVER SPRING, MARYLAND

Copyright © 2015 by Konstantin Kulakov

All rights reserved. This book or any portion thereof may not be reproduced or used in any manner whatsoever without the express written permission of the publisher except for the use of brief quotations in a book review.

Printed in the United States of America

Dialogue Foundation Books
An Imprint of Dialogue Foundation, Inc.
P.O. Box 10988
Silver Spring, MD 20914

ISBN-13: 978-0692466360

ISBN-10: 0692466363

Library of Congress Control Number: 2015915590

Illustrations: Adina-Larisa Sufana
Book design: Vanessa Maynard
Author photo: Jared Siskin

www.konstantinkulakov.com

For Lamar

ACKNOWLEDGEMENTS

I would like to thank the Dialogue Foundation for giving this work a home. I would also like to thank the following for their indispensible faith, support, or carefully written comments: Mikhail Kulakov, Lyudmila Kulakov, Sabrina Frometa, Olivia Minick, David Hegstad, Shelley Crook, Timothy Wotring, Kelly Maeshiro, Michael Crumpler, Daniel Aguilar, John Rogers, and Jaime Myers.

Thank you to the following for taking the time to personally illuminate their life-long commitment to the creation of poetry: Franz Wright, Bob Hicok, Ira Saddoff, Kazim Ali, Anne Becker.

Some of the poems have appeared or are forthcoming in the following publications: *Phoebe, Tule Review, Christian Century, Harvard Journal of African American Public Policy, Wildspice,* and *Tidal Basin Review.* The poem "If We Burn Them Altogether" has also been translated into Russian for the book *We're Just Standing on the Shore* by Eksmo Press in Moscow.

TABLE OF CONTENTS

I.

PERESTROIKA	12
KEATS BY GLENMONT METRO	14
SONG FOR EDEN IN D.C.	16
IF WE BURN THEM ALL TOGETHER	17
SHINING DARK	22
MORTON PEAK	23
MERTON IN BARDSTOWN	25
FACES OF STONE	26
DREAM FRAGMENT	28
EROS IN GEORGIA	29
SONG TO FLYING	31
IT IS HERE	34

II.

LORD, THIS DECEMBER, IN MY FLESH	38
WRISTBAND	40
SONG FOR DATING	42
WHERE PEOPLE MOVE AND FIND THEIR BEING	43
HAYWARD, WISCONSIN	46
THE GRASS IS GREENER...	47
PAINTING IN MY BATHROOM	49
EXCAVATING THE SKY	50
UNTITLED	53
KRASOTA SPASET MIR	54
END OF THE CENTURY	56

I.

PERESTROIKA

In the sterile-white room, I would look-out
the window and lose count in the snow.

After about 30 minutes, I would hear
Mom's keys rustle in the lock and see

her waist-long hair before my eyes.
She would carry a small aluminum can

and set it on the white table.
Slowly, she would tear open the metal.

Inside: a mango cut in halves, aglow.

KEATS BY GLENMONT METRO

I.

Metrorail. A spent, amber streetlight.
There, a deer tearing at warm grass—

a nauseous-sweet mist rising
as from a Bangladeshi garden. Tomorrow,

the sun will climb over its carcass
with two words from a whirring car: *road kill.*

II.

There is a house I cannot enter
at a certain time of day. Within its blank walls:

a sultry air of honey-spice, a clock, a sari
drying on a rack. I have sat there certain days

to slurp the curry. But not the nights when her mother
swells the house with the plume of spice,

not when her father washes and prays *Bismillah.*
I have only sent letters to her father and mother.

III.

Pricey liquor. On black-lit cushions: tan, half-hidden thighs.
Musty squad car seats, the scratch of dispatch.

In rented rooms, bottles of smoke to inhale
as you clutch for the fridge, propelling you into sleep.

Too near, too near is the rail to pull me there.
And not far from there, my grandfather beneath soil.

IV.

Tonight, I do not go there. Instead, I enter my home,
      my bed, and
let the landscape bleed-in: forbidden house,
      black-lit street, graveyard.

Behind shut eyes, I visit all the places. I take a rail, a car,
and for my grave, a not-so-heavy plummet and thud

on my scratched wooden floor, nursing thoughts of Grandpa—
still, I cannot see whether, tomorrow, armored tanks
      will roll down

my leafy avenue—or will it be the sameness of
      a forbidden house, a black-lit street, a graveyard?

SONG FOR EDEN IN D.C.

I am up, body heavy, pleading,
"Where's the gilt Eden I dreamed?"
Here, it's cement and rabid blinking
for her unearthly look, unredeemed.

Flesh and cents, flesh and cents, days
from crumbling to earth. All's healed,
but all's apart: skin tones, freeways
dissected by those falling to build.

"Lazy! Traitor!" they shout in their mob.
"Where are your documents?
Love without paper? Work without job?
All you fit in is moments."

But I'm just in search of high ground, DO NOT
DISTURBs hung from thin heavens,
singing, "when the sun does come 'round,
I'll depart from this island forever."

IF WE BURN

THEM ALL TOGETHER

I.

I say, "Never place one on top of the other."
At my bedside, the Qur'an lies not far from my Bible.

II.

Over cold salads, a woman fires out,
"And what the hell's the Qur'an?! The Bible is truth."

To our quick-drying sea of English phrases,
this ancient word comes

from the far, wispy guttural of the Arabic
Qir 'a, meaning "reading, recitation." It comes

only by name, a sound she mouths: *Koran*.

III.

This thin girl brought a heavy name
to my tongue. She told me, "I'm Muslim...

We read the Qur'an." And my ear snatched
this sound—a restless boy, entranced

by the look of dark eyes on the honey
of Bengali skin. Weeks later, dizzy from lust,

I spun my way into a bookstore, finding
Bible and Qur'an, side by side, to be taken.

IV.

"You know they cut off hands?" they told me.
"You know they slay infidels?" they added.

As I turned each, unread page,
I was a child in Arabia, uncovering

crumpled texts from sand. I imagined
a young Muhammad, thirteen centuries ago,

hearing Jibrael first whisper these words:
Recite in the name of your Lord who created—

created man from clots of blood.
Recite, and your Lord is the most Generous, -

who taught by the pen—
taught man that which He knew not.

V.

In Moscow, a man holds his bloodied forehead.
Front-page *Express* reads "Islamic Bombing."

In Baghdad, a man carries a just-severed head, crying,
"Allahu Akbar! Allahu Akbar!" through the blank room.

*Recite in the name of your Lord who created—
created man from clots of blood...*

I walk in my darkness and listen for the whisper.

VI.

We troll through the gleaming, yellow-green park.
"My dad was asking, 'What happened to us?

What happened to us Muslims?'" she tells me, smiling.
"'What happened to our empires, our science, math,

and art?'" I say nothing to this. Instead,
I cut her off and press on about class,

carrying the thoughts of my teacher:
"The more books we read from them,

the less likely we'll drop bombs on them."
I add, "If only we could break the code of Arabic...

If only we can read out dreams, each to each. If only..."

VII.

Tonight,

I watch crowds in Pakistan protest the Pope,
hailing the man who killed a scorned lawyer.

"He tried to change the law," says the imam
about the lawyer. "He's the Pope's agent," adds another.

I pace around my bed, consoling. Maybe now,
maybe now, I should start on my old, little project—

that untrodden region Keats told me about.
That room in my mind where, not far from the corner,

piles of thin wishes cover with dust. There,
above Qur'an and Bible, two different heavens

rise-up and conjoin: it is rivers of milk, streets
of gold, hairless companions, and pearly gates.

I leave these thin wishes as words on a page. Here,
at my bedside, the Qur'an lies not far from the Bible.

SHINING DARK

You, scheduled for chem lab,
but really here, luminous. You,

two green chili peppers
in your front shirt pocket. You,

praying in parking lots—not amen
but the Arabic amiiin. You,

digging hands into earth,
plopping out a mole. And one night,

face streaked black with tears
but shining dark—you.

MORTON PEAK

San Bernardino County

I.

Loose night: we pause. I close and open my eyes,
letting the deep-green nose-curve of a mountain

infuse my pupils in the chilled summer black:
minuscule buds and bushes—unknown by name—protrude,

dotting the immense slope like dying, electric bulbs.

II.

Still, there is nothing electric here; the city is beneath,
its burning streets a red-dressed whore to this light. I say,

"Redland lights, be gone! Don't fake the sun tonight!"
then quit the thought, imagining the chilled teeth

of a mountain cat: I see it raid the dark for its midnight meat.

III.

Like the waking dead, we pull ourselves to the heavens,
lugging thoughts: "God is real." "No. Superstition!"

Bodies heavy, I say, "The real Real is too traumatic
for any being to behold..." Thus, I cannot write the truth.

There will always be some kid-genius to *un*-write it
from his dark corner of earth. Let the mountain write.

IV.

At the peak, the air is refrigerated, the terrain:
planetary. But let me stand here for a smoke

of cold air. Height, sweat, beasts of old, come.
Watch the mountain murder these words.

MERTON IN BARDSTOWN

Thomas Merton (1915-1968), American writer and poet.
After abandoning a literary career in New York City, he joined
a Trappist Monastery in Bardstown, Kentucky.

At the window, a chill enters
from the green hills, swelling the room

with wisps of clean air. In my gut,
a dull tremor, after the steel ladle

nudges the bucket. My stomach is empty
save for a morsel of bread

gulped down with stream water.
I write how flowers of blood

nailed Christ to the walls of Harlem.

FACES OF STONE

I.

Christ Church College, Oxford, 1995

A boy, in black, plays on white steps,
jumping. The face of stone: changed.

I ask, "How many feet shuffled past here
to wear deep grooves into rock?" Dad says,

"It is not the feet you count. It takes time; it takes time—"

II.

Montgomery Blair, Maryland, 2007

Once, in a hallway, I was struck by strange beauty.
And tonight, in kitchen light, deep

in her dark Bengali features,
I see her parents and their faces of smooth stone.

Stone, stone. For her tradition is inherited, stone-deep.
Useless rock or decoration, it is carried; it is worn.

III.

Forbidden Home

After dinner, she spoke the unspeakable,
a mass of softened words with wings: "I love him."

The words rose above her parents, their walls, their car,
casting a stone-silence for months. Each week, I say,

"How many times will you walk past their bedroom
before a smile cracks thin through their stone?" She says,

"It is not the walks you count. It takes time; it takes time—"

IV.

Shaw Avenue

Tonight,

I imagine that Oxford stone. I imagine, too,
her mother—hushed-still as limestone—and her father

in the bedroom—motionless as a Greek statue.
Still, one evening, when she pled with her mother,

I remember she said—face of flesh or face of stone—
her mother broke. A tear-drop in the stone.

DREAM FRAGMENT

Breaking through the wave, a honey-
colored sun in abyssal blue. I lean

behind the plane's window and turn my body
toward the woman I love.

As I turn back, the wave rises above
the plane's belly, the sun a streak as bright

as Christ and the city beneath
now jolting at us while I grab her hand.

EROS IN GEORGIA

"The little love god lying once asleep..."
- Sonnet 154

The moon is an aluminum pan!
And the clouds pull over it

like muslin in a high school play.
Somewhere, leaning off a stone balcony,

I breathe and let my eyes to the blackness—

God! The deep of the wood is too green!
Not far from my left, blanketed with branches,

I hear a girl's easy laughter unloose.
The Verona-like water of a swimming pool

expels its hot breath. And from some box,
a country singer pulls his heavy drawl

while his name stays unknown.

The girl's laugh spreads far. It's tended by
a deeper song: a boy, glad in her softness.

And I know there is the running, the asking,
the speaking their names and histories,

but in this minute, in this Eros-stricken air,
let them be the earth-held paradise

of moon-skimmed water, sex, and youth.

SONG TO FLYING

I.

In a sky-colored dress—with longish black curls
you scour behind pale American houses,

praying to Allah for some sick bird to catch
and cup in your palms: you will make it fly.

II.

In a neat English playground, near a worn brick sidewalk,
I mumble in mixed Russian, digging

pale hands into earth, burying sticks and rocks:
a time capsule to call mine in a far-off adulthood.

III.

In a small greenish bookshop, as you left
for the restroom, a dizzy happiness

came to my chest. In minutes, you'd hear of my love and,
looking away, say: "Stop thinking with your body."

IV.

Strict scholars invent laws. With the stroke of a pen,
they prohibit our love. Your father denies meetings,

so we touch in metro corners, telling ourselves:
"They worship religion; their God is locked into words."

V.

But this morning I tell you, "Let's marry; let's go to Jamaica;
I will build us a mosque and a church. There

our children will catch starfish and eat jackfruit;
they will bow to a God that commands us to love."

VILLAGE CHRISTIAN

After the last power line falls with a flare,
after the last cable comes down, clean,
after the last inch drowns the road with snow,
you are alone. Nothing but the soon-gone comfort

of laptops, cell phones, flashlights:
a lifespan of a common bathroom fly.
I am afraid. I am no longer the prince-God
with a car. The gas is working, so I bathe

in the hot dark. The mind turns to villages
and their warm, rustling prayers.

I would walk the snow for her.
I would walk the snow for her. How I pray
she isn't dead-cold in some cold ditch.

I speak this prayer like a village Christian.

IT IS HERE

I.

Post-Soviet Russia

Each time she threw clean bedcovers
on my Russian bed, I was in England.

The blue Tank Engine would unfold his smile,
burying the mud roads behind my window.

On my nightstand, the Oxford reading lamp
breathed-in an air of Western comfort.

And I would lie as images of America
rose to the ceiling above my bunk bed.

II.

Ino, Wisconsin

Our first house sprawled out in the green,
the precise plastic boards exalted in the sun.

Entering the mall, the rows opened like
the gates of true communism or Zion.

The drive-thru dining, mothered in the city,
served neat meals to the barest of corners.

Even at the dentist, I did not know pain, only
a mask on my nose and the shifting of panels.

III.

Northwestern High School, South Carolina

Many days, I thought late into the darkness,
nursing dying dreams of flashbulb triumph.

Many days, I floated through pale school halls,
threatened only by the monsters of fashion.

I learned life is a mute, gentle oppression
lined with rails near the edges of peril.

IV.

The first time I saw it, I was twenty,
escaping to the woods with friends of friends.

Below my feet: an earth-colored reservoir
filled a crater blown deep in the ground. There,

they jumped into the waters, inches
from striking the stone, the stone.

There was no guardrail, no police; just
pale-orange boulders—and then the water.

V.

Tonight,

I see the evening separating along
its seams: near the bedcovers,

the guardrails, and the lights, the steel,
the mud roads, and the pain hover.

It is here. It was present all along.

II.

LORD, THIS DECEMBER, IN MY FLESH

Lord, this December, in my flesh
a thorn. Thank You for the thorn.

I rise. A sheet of ice has fallen
from my eyes. Thank You for the thorn.

I see now. When I speak Your Name,
I name Eternity. Thank You for the thorn.

WRISTBAND

I.

The first time I met Jabar,
November stripped the city gray—

a bus waited anonymously
with only the last free seat.

Then, I didn't know, to face a stranger
was to fling-open a separate world:

it was just the weight upon our faces,
the bearing it, the "I will make it work."

II.

By February, his cancer came back;
my love life swung from its orbit.

Now, I would bring wine to a home
filled with chicken, rice, and steam.

There was no talk of pending test results.
Only *The Haves and the Have Nots* until

he asked me to call, mouthed
"colon removal," began to cry.

III.

For weeks, I dreaded visiting him,
dreaded the impotence of words:

"Hi, Jabar. I just wanted to say
that there is nothing I can say."

March began to turn the city green.

IV.

When I came to his room,
he was not there. I only

heard his voice down the hall
as he cheered on other patients.

To prognosis, he said he does not know.
"Great people here," he continued. "Look—

a boy gave me a red wristband… Isn't that crazy?
He guessed my favorite color: red."

SONG FOR DATING

Hit the switch;
turn off the dreams.
Hope is tricky
between lovers' seats.

Burnt, homeless souls,
lovers without love.
Where can you go
when everywhere's home?

Scanning radio waves,
staring at her eyes.
I never caught a soul;
I only got a piece.

Now string the bits together
and call this thing your life.
Tonight it's only wires
that hold me all in one.

WHERE PEOPLE MOVE AND FIND THEIR BEING

*"The projects in Harlem are hated...
And they are hated for the same reason:
both reveal, unbearably, the real attitude
of the white world..."
- James Baldwin*

I.

Jamaica Center, Queens

First, it is the bodega, blossoming
with a ruffle of coats and lotto tickets.

The liquor store, pale-green,
yet empty in the street.

The young, weathered faces
enthroned on gray stoops.

The thin church walls, trembling
to "Peace in the valley"—and an

unendurable grayness, crying-out,
"Lose hope; we have abandoned you."

II.

They tell me,

"You can say the word 'injustice,'
but cannot know the weight

of body rejected, the hot flush

of father arrested. You can read

the word 'shooting,' but cannot know
the crackle of gun shots,

the teeth against cement—"
here, at the edges of peril where

people move and find their being.

III.

Harlem

This is how those with much
take from those with little:

Slowly, the metallic bodega
is cleared for the dim bar.

The small handle is sawed-off
for the brass revolving door.

They say, "This is Morningside Heights!
The edges of peril are not near!

The thug, the prostitute: gone!,
pushed further from our luster."

IV.

Still, in the pregnancy of night, two Angels
broke through the skyline. Lifting

the blackness, they say: "No! the one you call
'crack whore' is the Blessed Mother; see her blue

garment, the dip of her brown breast.
She is holy." Then, revealing a man

in an side street, another Seraph advances:

"No," she says, hovering. "The son you call thug,

the son plummeting in bullets, is The Christ…" And,
illuminating his vast body, says "He is

the fabric of existence… Repent, repent…"

V.

After the decision is proclaimed, those
in whiter spaces sink into their beds.

Outside, like burning petals, an expanding line
of youth, streams into the night.

Signing hands-ups and I-can't-breathes,
they make-real their Last Supper.

While, in the streets, the armored tanks
wait beneath a blackening sky.

HAYWARD, WISCONSIN

I did not fish in Lake Superior but
brought bluegills from the pond to fry.

It was a warmer place after Moscow, though
in my yard I never dug up that longed-for

turtle or gold chest. Up the street: the kids
I paid in coins to be my friends. And there was also

the school where, one night, a native girl
lit-up my twelve-year-old heart.

On the last day of school, I vowed I would
hug her goodbye. It was too late, though.

Two months later, I left for Rock Hill, South Carolina—
an emptiness heavier than longing itself.

THE GRASS IS GREENER...

How horrid it would be to unclasp
this life and all the love in it.
Yet, how horrid it would be to breathe
immortal while centuries, centuries fall

like Beauvoir's burnt-out Fosca.

PAINTING IN MY BATHROOM

I.

I emerge to see a face, distinct
from the cloud-like steam

of the shower. It is a little girl:
a ballerina in a purple dress.

II.

Soft eyes. Too many times
I have walked past her look

to wash, brush teeth,
empty the drain with yellow.

I say, "Five years, you have hung, hook-high,
your endless look unnoticed."

III.

I stand in the rush of steam;
I say, "Before the replica

was hung, before the oil
was printed, before the girl

was buried as a woman, she stood:
her soft eyes and purple dress."

EXCAVATING THE SKY

I.

I would excavate the sky of clouds
to know you, Yahweh. Yahweh,

my nails are black with soil;
I am rummaging for Your holy light.

Yahweh, thunder, storm deity,
I no longer fear you. I have spoken

the unspeakable name: Yahweh.

II.

Once, you placed sweet thorns
in my leg and in my groin

to make me weak, to bring me
near to You. Now, as an open fridge

in an abandoned lot,
my earth is empty of Your spirit. Now,

Your silence is absurd as wreckage,
and my body is empty of Your spirit.

III.

Each morning, I rise like
the wrestling Jacob, running

through parking lots. I pray,
"Break open my counting brain;

make me your holiest fool."
What blessed psych ward

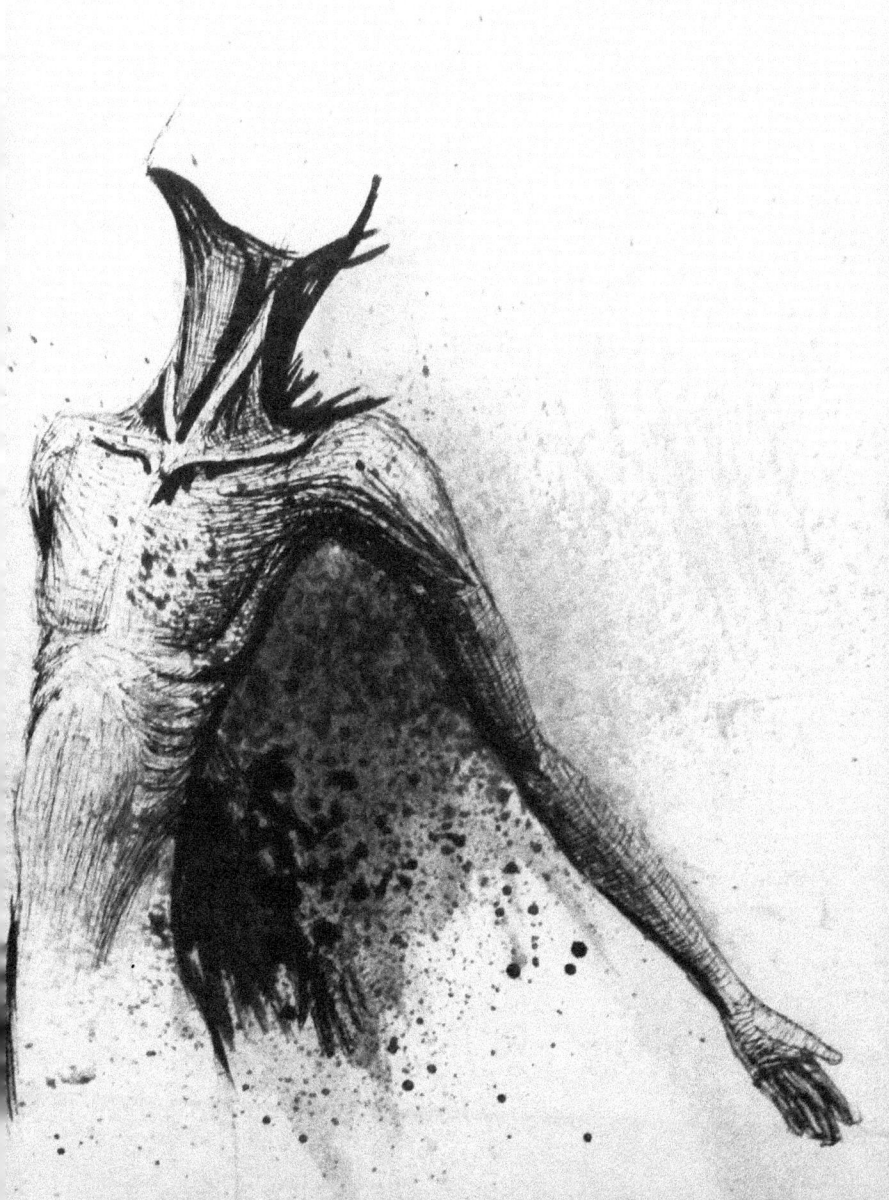

must they leadeth me to...

IV.

Aquinas, broken, in the Lux Aeterna,
Blake seeing God through his window,

Ginsberg in his East Village flat,
trapping the archangel of the soul.

I walk into my future; no vision in my pocket.

V.

But this winter night, my feet touch
chilled cement in honor

of firm gravity. Near the porch
a girl invites me to the economy

of tenderness. I run a bath where
visions rise like lavender steam

above my skull. In my room,
I punch in letters, mixing words

to bring-out sparks. And it is You, Yahweh.

I.

By the car, in the wet black,
        I could not close
                the umbrella until
        I did, its body folding and unfolding
                like a deep-sea jellyfish.

II.

                The police beacons
flashed and wailed; they did not want
        to go to bed.
                To them I said,
"The rain will shush and lull
        you all to sleep.
                And it will fall
        like glass shavings
                from YHWH's workshop."

KRASOTA SPASET MIR

*"Beauty will save the world
(Krasota spaset mir)."*
- Prince Myskin, <u>The Idiot</u>

I.

Your russet tresses fall,
a clockwork lightness where

your skin blends sheens of
chestnut and bronze. I am

wounded: you have opened
your eyes, splitting the air

with depth and precision.

II.

You lie before me, drawing
back your hair like a svelte branch

in dry wind; I advance
toward your neck and breathe in.

There, beneath your ear: a
fading scent assaults me.

III.

Tension. Your body folds
and unfolds; skin brushes

against skin, burning like
hot vents beneath

a seabed: *krasota spaset mir.*

IV.

Outside, the traffic has
died down. A light rain falls

like scratches on a
black mirror. The sky

opens itself to be seen.

V.

I am within you, heavy,
a part of me collapsing

into the tender of you. There,
at your dissolute core,

your mouth and rib cage opening:
krasota spaset mir.

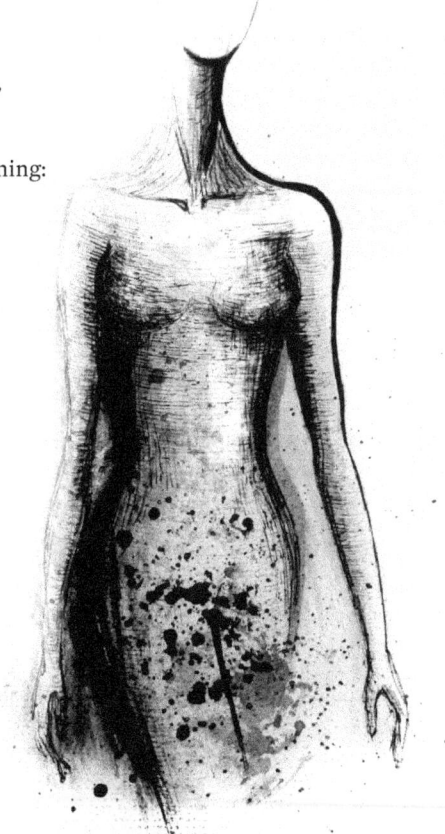

END OF THE CENTURY

I.

Your Wisdom spoke energy into matter,
    spinning stardust into precise earths.

It is written into each twig that breaks into
    blossom, each pupil that soaks-in light.

It secured for intellect and freedom
    to rise-up from Darwin's unshorn brute.

Tzelem Elohim, Imago Dei:
    the only image of Yourself is us.

II.

Now, at the heart of Your city, there rests
a large golden calf. It shines fat, exalted

by glass towers and lifted high by metal spires.
Near the outskirts, power plants sprawl out,

poisoning Your streams, blackening Your clouds.
Beneath the gray, Your weak wake early,

pushed out each morning—to lift up the skyline.
While in the streets, the steel holding our cars

bolts us from each other's tender space.
O, send down your judgment! Destroy our calf!

III.

Each night, locked behind doors, we push ideas
into your silence. From our mouths,

there rise words, words, words, stretching
ferric walls of thought to hide Your blessed light.

Now, a newspaper column, a Bible verse
hold-up Your broken city, and with a turn

of phrase, we make worlds that we can live in.
While through the windows, we cannot see

the structure trembling in our streets.
O, smash the idol! Know the living God!

IV.

Tonight, I saw the end of this century:
with Your earth never as hot, we raised

red Gehenna from its depths ourselves.
All for the gold, all for the luster,

we have run down the ice caps, sinking
buildings under water. Now, the glass towers

lie barred shut; the ATMs are drowned.
Now, the idol of religion lies lopsided,

and the churches are cleared and sold for lots.
O, they have failed to give-forth Your light!

V.

Still, for generations, a small band of persons
inherits the earth. In violet-gray dusk,

they scour the damp offices; they stalk
the ruined fields. Like the prophets, they take

to the wilderness. There, looking out toward
the opening sky, they renew their vows to Reality.

Never again will ideas, ideas, ideas assault
Your Beauty; never will language oppress. Now,

they will know each time the word "I" is spoken,
a fresh leaf shrinks and falls from Your Eden.

www.ingramcontent.com/pod-product-compliance
Lightning Source LLC
Chambersburg PA
CBHW051703040426
42446CB00009B/1284